NONVIOLENT COMMUNICATION AT WORK

How to communicate productively in challenging situations

Written by Véronique Bronckart
Translated by Carly Probert

NONVIOLENT COMMUNICATION AT WORK

- **Problem**: What attitude should be adopted in order to use nonviolent communication in business?
- **Uses:** Preventing violence, addressing conflictual situations constructively, promoting collaboration and optimising professional relations.
- **Professional context:** Professional relations, team management, teamwork, personal and professional development.
- **FAQs:**
  - What is nonviolent communication?
  - How can nonviolent communication help me?
  - Is nonviolent communication helpful in the case of conflict?
  - How can I set up a process of nonviolent communication?
  - Who is involved in nonviolent communication?
  - How can nonviolent communication impact my professional life?

Whether in our personal or professional lives, we all eventually face various kinds of tensions. Involving opposing interests or different viewpoints between people, conflict – which is often emotionally charged – deserves our attention. Although it is far from pleasant, conflict can be useful as long as we learn to communicate and bring out the positives in the situation: indeed, through conflict we learn, we change and we build our relationships with others.

Yet all too often we tend to adopt a bad attitude towards these disputes. This can result in even more negative consequences than the initial conflict: relational, physical or psychological violence directed towards others or against ourselves. But why do we act in this way? How can we learn not to react instinctively when faced with a disagreement? How can we optimise our social and professional rela- tionships to enable us to work together peacefully?

Try using nonviolent communication to seek rational and constructive responses to your relationship problems. Get yourself out of the vicious cycle of unhealthy exchanges marked by anger, revenge and violence, and become aware of your feelings, desires and actions!

THE KEY TO NONVIOLENT COMMUNICATION AT WORK

WHAT IS NONVIOLENT COMMUNICATION?

A question of terminology

Communicating non-violently implies that the speaker shows empathy, compassion, cooperation and respect towards the person they are addressing. They are caring towards themselves and towards others. The term "non-violence" was popularised by Gandhi's (Indian spiritual guide, 1869-1948) movement and referred, at the time, to interacting with one another without causing harm. This concept is based on two assumptions:

- all individuals experience basic needs;
- each of them is able to accommodate others.

Definition

Nonviolent Communication (NVC) is a registered trademark that brings together concepts and methods developed by American psychologist Marshall B. Rosenberg (1934-2015) in the 1960s. He defined it as a mode of communication involving language, thinking and skills in terms of communication, whilst allowing the individual to stay true to themselves. It involves two parts – the "self" and the "other" – and is organised around four essential steps based on observation, feeling, need and demand.

EXTRA INFORMATION

To avoid using the term "violence", which can sometimes be misinterpreted, we also speak of conscious or empathetic communication.

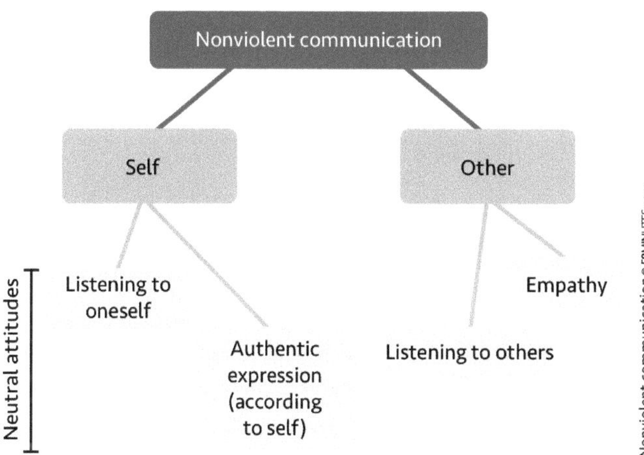

The goal is to improve communication through the development of neutral attitudes, such as listening, observing and identifying your own feelings and needs, as well as those of others. But beware, this does not mean establishing rules that must be followed at all costs, but understanding and establishing benchmarks that will teach you to express yourself in a caring manner.

What is its purpose?

> We have all learned to speak, but not necessarily to communicate. Our relationships too often degenerate into power relationships, whether in our personal or professional lives.

Given these findings, nonviolent communication teaches us to analyse the behaviours, needs and desires of one another and to better express them. Thus, it improves our way of communicating and resolving conflicts constructively and positively, by negotiating compromises and thus fighting against rivalry and favouring collaboration. To do this, it uses assertiveness based on authenticity, which means daring to express how we feel and what we want deep down in order to meet our own needs and values, while preventing our unconscious emotions, such as shame, guilt or duty, from resurfacing.

Establishing this practice in a company helps to improve the welfare of the individuals within it and, consequently, their performances. It is especially useful in times of stress and crisis. These are indeed key moments, during which managers and employees need to communicate positively to build relationships of trust and cooperate satisfactorily.

Nonviolent communication limits power games and soothes tensions within the team. Meanwhile, it re-motivates individuals and clarifies your relationship to yourself when you are overwhelmed with emotion.

Impact of nonviolent communication

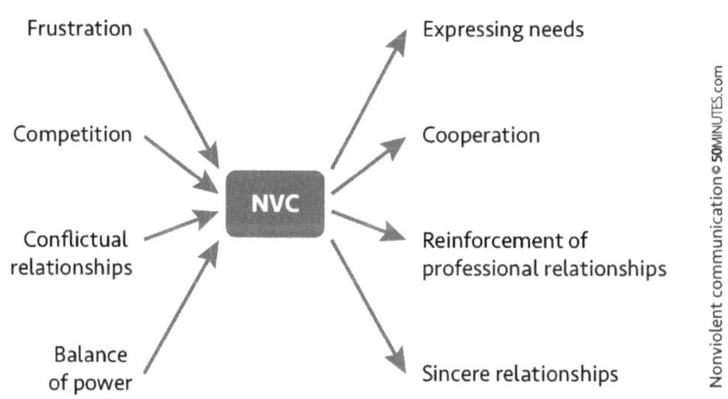

THE STAGES OF NONVIOLENT COMMUNICATION

Four phases are necessary for the success of nonviolent communication in conflict resolution: observing, expressing feelings, expressing needs and asking. It is important to follow this path.

Observing

The first step is to observe a fact or a specific behaviour that affects our wellbeing. This allows us to consider the situation objectively and without judgment, and to question what bothers us. This means we can identify different things, such as:

- objective observations (which could be detected without drawing conclusions)
- assessments
- interpretations.

These last two are legitimate and can be expressed, as long as it is made clear that they are subjective and not real. Therefore, they should be distinguished from objective observations. It is advisable not to carry any real judgment on the person, for risk of offending them, which would bring any discussions to an end.

Recommended formulations:
"I've noticed that the report is not finished yet". Here, we focus on an observed fact. Conversely, the remark "I see that you have not finished the report yet" can be seen as a personal criticism with an underlying message such as "You are taking too long on that report", "It is your fault", etc.
Again, "Your files are not organised" will be better received than "You are really disorganised, you leave your files everywhere!".
Finally, "I noticed that your sales figures were lower this week" is preferable to "You did not deliver good sales figures

> this week!", because that sentence makes a judgement on the abilities of the other person.

It is also important to recognise and distinguish between the different types of conflict:

- **Conflict of interest**. An individual has multiple interests that come into opposition and can affect the motivation of others.
- **Power struggle.** Everyone tries to increase their power at the expense of others.
- **Relationship conflict.** People do not have the same definition of their relationship.
- **Emotional conflict.** Individuals have opposing feelings or emotions.
- **Cultural conflict.** People have different views, values, thoughts or ways of life.

Being able to identify these problems means you can better confront them. As you will read in the next chapter, there is no single effective way to deal with these different situations: we must constantly adapt.

THINGS TO AVOID

Don't stay in a power struggle or competition without any real intention of communicating these observations.

Expressing feelings

In this second step, you should identify your feelings following this, and express them by separating them from your interpretations and your prejudices. Nonviolent communication invites you to develop your emotional intelligence, to explore and share your feelings (of surprise, curiosity, fear, frustration, sadness, etc.). It is crucial to listen to yourself and understand what you are feeling and why. By getting to know and asserting yourself, you will succeed in getting others to understand you. Indeed, it is easier for the other person to improve their behaviour if they are aware of its impact on you. It is also important to let others express their emotions.

> Recommended formulations:
> "I noticed that the report is not yet completed and that worries me because…"
> "I see that your files are not organised, this annoys me because…"
> "I noticed that your sales figures fell this week. This concerns me because…"

ADVICE

Don't be afraid to reveal your feelings on account of modesty or fear of the judgment of others. Assertiveness is the first step in finding solutions to meet your expectations. By hiding what you feel, you will only postpone the problem.

Expressing needs

We usually think that situations or events are the cause of our emotions and attitudes. However, we often don't realise that our needs are an intermediate link between our feelings and the behaviours of others. It is important to recognise, accept and express needs, frustrations and feelings. They are revealed spontaneously by our emotions (fear, anger, sadness, etc.) and can trigger a "mirror" effect on the person you are speaking to. By arousing their empathy, you can more easily find common ground. Nonviolent communication is inconceivable without exchange or active and empathetic listening to individual needs.

> Recommended formulations:
> "I noticed that the report is not yet completed and that worries me, because I have to meet with the client this afternoon and I would like to discuss it with him…"
> "I see that your files are not organised, this annoys me because we find it difficult to find each project…"
> "I noticed that your sales figures fell this week. This concerns me because the monthly goals will not be achieved…"

The obstacles to expressing our needs can be diverse in nature: education, social or family context in which we grow up, shyness, fear of not knowing what word to use to best express feelings and needs, the fear of being criticised or misunderstood, etc.

Asking

Now it is time to make your request in a concrete, realistic and positive manner. An open request, without requirement but negotiable, allows you to switch more easily to action and meeting individual needs. Formulating your needs at that time – i.e. after the first three phases – makes it negotiable. Do not show yourself as overly aggressive, demanding, threatening, authoritarian or manipulative, as this may cause fear or frustration for the other person.

> Recommended formulations
> "Could you finish this report by noon so I can discuss it during my appointment with the client this afternoon? That way we can close the case earlier."
> "Could you organise your files today so that we can find our way in the current projects? It will save us a lot of time."
> "I noticed that your sales figures fell this week. This concerns me because the monthly goals will not be achieved. Do you think you can straighten the curve before the end of the week to avoid financial losses?"

In order for the request to be heard, it must be:

- **Active and positive,** because it is important to ask for what you want, instead of what you do not want.
- **Conscious and explicit,** to avoid any misinterpretation.
- **Simple, clear and precise,** so that it is well understood.
- **Free of any form of authoritarianism** or a request using "you must" or "you have to", in order to prevent the submission or rebellion of the other person.

Extra information

Listening to and welcoming the remarks of others with kindness and without judgement is one of the key points of nonviolent communication.

GIRAFFE VS. JACKAL

As part of nonviolent communication, Marshall B. Rosenberg includes two animals to illustrate our attitudes towards others:

- The giraffe is the symbol of nonviolent communication. With a big heart and tall stature, the giraffe quickly glances at what is going on around him. In the context of nonviolent communication, these two features (benevolence and height) allow him to take a step back to analyse difficult situations and plan long-term actions. He is empathetic, speaks honestly, openly expresses his feelings and listens to those of others. He represents the language of the heart and his goal is to create a serene and respectful relationship with others.

  > Giraffe language example: "When your records are not organised, it annoys me because I lose so much time trying to find the one I want. Could you put them in the right place?"

- The jackal (or wolf) is in a power struggle. He diagnoses, judges, classifies, labels and demands. He tends to want to control others by manipulating or playing with their feelings. He represents violence in a relationship, because his language is based on judgement, criticism, manipulation and domination. Too often this leads to confrontation and conflict.

Jackal language example: "You drive me mad when you do not organise your files! You don't really respect your colleagues and I waste so much time trying to find what I need. But you seem to find it normal!"

PATHS TO NONVIOLENT COMMUNICATION

To get a clearer idea of what a nonviolent communication process really means, try to put yourself in some of the situations described below. For each, specific solutions are suggested.

Obstacle	The right attitude
The other person is dishonest.	Calmly increase your questions in order to make them talk and identify their contradictions. Then, state that their behaviour does not seem compatible with searching for a solution. Make your needs clear.
The other person systematically criticises you.	Welcome criticism calmly. Listen to the other person, without arguing against what they say. Try to understand their true intention. Refuse to be labelled and ask for concrete evidence. Recognise the criticisms that seem concrete and respond to those that are not.
The other person is aggressive.	Keep your cool. Listen, but do not show any indulgence. Take things in hand without showing your determination. Try to determine what lies behind this attitude (uncertainty, lack of confidence, need for recognition, etc.). Allow them to externalise their anger, as long as it does not cross the limits of being acceptable. If you feel insulted or physically threatened, interrupt the conversation. Once their anger has subsided, let them know that you are not their enemy and want to sincerely find a common solution. Use "we" to show them that they are involved in the resolution of the problem.
The other person does not engage.	Do not give up and think that the cause is lost. If the other person is doing this, it is probably because they have difficulty communicating and expressing their emotions, or are indecisive. Ask them questions, reassure them and encourage them to come forward. Be warm and avoid pushing them to take part.
The other person seems shocked.	"What? Something's wrong between us? If I'd known…". Either they are feigning ignorance, or they really did not know there was a problem. Detail the situation methodically, giving precise facts and examples and use nonviolent communication techniques to help them understand the problem.

Obstacle	The right attitude
The other person is incoherent.	Incessant chatter, scattered thoughts; the other person has trouble putting forward and organising their ideas. Keep calm and do not waste your energy unnecessarily. Focus the discussion on your mutual goals and pause, giving partial syntheses to highlight each positive proposal. Make sure the other follows you in this approach. Be reassuring and sure of yourself.
The other person is focused on themselves.	They complain, dwell on their personal efforts and insist on their needs without considering yours. They will not listen to you and the only solution they find satisfactory is the one they put forward. Do not become annoyed and insist on the need to find a solution together. Do not be pressured into accepting a conclusion too quickly, just to "keep the peace". Alternatively, let them know that if you both remain stubborn and focused on your own objectives, you will never find a solution.
The other person is anxious.	They act dramatically and beat themselves up. Help them to focus on objective facts and take the heat out of the conflict. Strive to follow a pragmatic approach and propose a method of work and a timescale. Show them you trust them and you are convinced that a solution is possible.
The other person refuses to talk.	What right does a person have to prevent you from expressing yourself freely? Try to learn more through questioning. If all communication is impossible, the relationship is unfortunately compromised as you cannot force someone to exchange with you.

DURING THE EXCHANGE

- Do not use "you", as this gives an accusatory tone to your sentence.
- Do not judge and do not criticise.
- Do not give orders or threaten.

- **Denying the conflict**: By being in denial, you transmit the image of a proud person ("We are too good a team to have conflicts") or a fearful or lost person ("I hate arguments and prefer not to acknowledge them"). If you act this way, you may see the conflict reappear later. Acceptance is the first step towards a resolution.
- **Resigning when faced with conflict:** By giving up, you reveal a lack of self-confidence or a weak character, who doesn't wish to intervene in a dispute. There is a chance that the people around you will see you as too nice, which will never allow you to manage the conflict.
- **Being physically or psychologically violent:** In doing this, you may give the impression of wanting to dominate and finding pleasure in the conflict. Be aware that violent confrontation can only make things worse. It reveals resentment and a desire for revenge.
- **Making judgements:** This can hurt the other person and close the dialogue. Therefore, remain neutral and base your thinking on facts. For example, instead of saying "You are not fully involved", say "I sensed that you were unmotivated by the last task I gave to you".

TOP TIPS

- Stay calm and open to discussion.
- Identify the source of conflict or disagreement.
- Talk about the situation using "I", not "you". Keep to formulations such as "I do not feel that you supported me in this task", rather than "You never help me". Also, use "we" when discussing the solutions.
- Identify and express your feelings, paying attention to the terms used which do not explicitly define your emotions. We often tend to express ourselves through phrases such as "I feel that…". However, these are more representative of our understanding of the behaviour of others. For example, instead of saying "I feel that you abandoned me", say "I feel abandoned and that makes me upset".
- Acknowledge and express your fears in the discussion. We tend to hide them, but this prevents us from recognising our real needs and therefore finding a solution.
- Justify and explain your needs so that they are understood. For example, "I want you to arrive on time because I interpret your delay as a lack of respect".
- Be kind and listen to others.
- Negotiate concrete and useful actions for the benefit of everyone.
- Be clear about your requests but avoid giving orders. For example, instead of saying "Starting tomorrow, I want you to organise all of these files", say "Could you take charge of organising these files from tomorrow?".

For this process to actually work, two things are necessary:

- For the other person to pay attention and listen;
- A desire to welcome dialogue and cooperation.

FAQS

WHAT IS NONVIOLENT COMMUNICATION?

Nonviolent communication is a communication process based on empathy and respect for ourselves and for others. It promotes understanding and acceptance of messages, in a caring and tolerant environment between two opposing parties. It is the result of a combination of verbal communication, body language, a way of thinking and know-how in communication. Each individual must observe the facts without judgement, differentiate feelings from interpretations and express their deepest needs to formulate a concrete and achievable request for the benefit of both parties, and of the company.

HOW CAN NONVIOLENT COMMUNICATION HELP ME?

The purpose of nonviolent communication is to improve our relationships with others in a constructive and positive way and to resolve conflicts by arousing empathy, compassion and communicating respectfully. By getting to know and understand each other, we gain confidence and boost wellbeing. Better communication within a company limits power games and competition and promotes cooperation. The whole team and its performance will benefit greatly from this method. It is also recommended as part of burnout prevention.

IS NONVIOLENT COMMUNICATION HELPFUL IN THE CASE OF CONFLICT?

You can use nonviolent communication in two ways:

- Communicating with yourself to understand what is happening within, i.e. self-empathy;
- Communicating with each other to resolve a conflictual situation.

In the first case, nonviolent communication involves being conscious of your "being", your "knowing", your emotions, your needs and your values, in order to act and assert yourself, without being disappointed or misunderstood by others. In the second case, it involves mutual respect and empathy, leading to healthy and positive professional relationships.

HOW CAN I SET UP A PROCESS OF NONVIOLENT COMMUNICATION?

To make use of this method, follow these four essential steps:

- observe facts and behaviour;
- identify and express the feelings experienced;
- recognise and express needs and fears;
- clearly express requests and actions.

WHO IS INVOLVED IN NONVIOLENT COMMUNICATION?

Nonviolent communication is for anyone who wants to improve their relationship with themselves and others, whether in a personal or professional context. This can be especially beneficial if you have trouble controlling your emotions or you react aggressively during a conflict.

HOW CAN NONVIOLENT COMMUNICATION IMPACT MY PROFESSIONAL LIFE?

Within your company, the benefits of nonviolent communication can be numerous:

- improve working relationships;
- strengthen collaboration between colleagues;
- motivate teams;
- reduce stress;
- boost self-confidence and assertiveness.

OVER TO YOU

Before adopting a nonviolent communication approach, you must first ask yourself about your current operations, in order to identify the areas that need your attention and which can be improved. Then, make an effort to practice the method outlined earlier. Be diplomatic when expressing your feelings and needs.

EXERCISE 1 – CURRENT BEHAVIOUR

When you disagree with someone in a situation, how do you behave? Enter a cross in the columns that correspond to your actions.

	Always	Rarely	Never
I try to gain the upper hand over the other person.			
I try to find a compromise with the other person.			
I mock, laugh and joke.			
I am silent and turn my back.			
I avoid the problem.			
I make the other person understand that I do not like their behaviour.			
I ask for help from other people.			
I ask for advice from other people.			
I threaten and blackmail.			
I verbally attack people.			
I express my feelings (pain, sadness, anger).			
I give in and let the other person win.			
I put decisions off until later.			
I want a solution as soon as possible.			
I give as good as I get and put the other person in their place.			
I cry and feel sorry for myself.			
I don't say anything, but go and cry at my desk.			
I get angry and claim things are unfair.			

Analyse your responses to identify your weak points and complete the exercises below.

If you think of other behaviours, list them here:

....

....

....

....

....

What comes to mind when you hear the following words?

Violence – Conflict – Aggression

....

....

....

....

EXERCISE 2 – PUTTING NONVIOLENT COMMUNICATION INTO PRACTICE

Imagine that you are in conflict with someone. Answer the following questions:

- What event triggers the urge to speak in both people? Describe the facts objectively.
- How do you feel? Identify your emotions and those of the other person.
- What needs do your emotions reflect? Avoid assigning blame and do not act defensively.
- What specific actions are expected by both people in or-

der to feel fulfilled? Are you willing to do this to solve the situation? Do not use threats, orders or manipulation.

EXERCISE 3 – SELF-EVALUATION

Complete the table below:

I am able to...	Yes	No	Skills to develop
Approach conflict calmly.			
Express myself honestly.			
Distinguish between observations, judgement and evaluations.			
Identify and express my feelings and needs.			
Formulate a clear, concrete and realistic request.			
Dare to confront the other person.			
Invite another person to discuss.			
Accept what another tells me.			
Listen to another with empathy.			
Understand the requests of others.			
Adjust my approach according to the reactions of others.			
Differentiate between the person and their behaviour.			
Face physical or moral violence.			

FURTHER READING

BIBLIOGRAPHY

- Rosenberg, M. (2006) Dénouer les conflits par la Communication NonViolente. Saint-Julien-en-Genevois: Éditions Jouvence.
- Rosenberg, M. (2003) La Communication NonViolente au quotidian. Saint-Julien-en-Genevois: Éditions Jouvence.

ADDITIONAL SOURCES

- Bronckart, V. (2015) *Comment donner et recevoir un feed-back constructif ?* Brussels: Lemaitre.
- Keller, F. (2013) *Pratiquer la CNV au travail. La communication NonViolente, passeport pour réconcilier bien-être et performance.* Paris: InterEditions.
- Myers, W. (2007) *Pratique de la Communication Non Violente : Etablir de nouvelles relations.* Saint-Julien-en-Genevois: Éditions Jouvence.
- CNV Belgique (2016) L'Association pour la Communication NonViolente de Belgique Francophone. [online]. [Accessed 8th August 2016] Available from:<http://cnvbelgique.be/>
- Van Stappen, A. (2015) Petit cahier d'exercices de Communication NonViolente. Illustrated by Jean d'Augagneur. Saint-Julien-en-Genevois: Éditions Jouvence.

50MINUTES.com

IMPROVE YOUR GENERAL KNOWLEDGE

IN A BLINK OF AN EYE !

www.50minutes.com

www.50minutes.com

Ebook EAN: 9782806279262

Paperback EAN: 9782806284211

Legal Deposit: D/2016/12603/367

Cover: © Primento

Digital conception by Primento, the digital partner of publishers.